THE COLORS OF PAIN
Wounded
Has Wounds Become Us?

Kamisha A. Oliver

Copyright © 2022 by Kamisha A. Oliver
All rights reserved.

To Sadie, my granddaughter,
in hopes that she will continue to think deeply,
love accountably and challenge that which needs
challenging.

And to Milan, my granddaughter,
in hopes that she will acknowledge the value of
having an older sibling whose footprints will create a path
that will become a map of what to do and what not to do.

And to Nyla, my granddaughter, in hopes that she
will be that much more secure in her path due to the
health of the generational standard being set.

As the lineage grows, I know that my life has been
dedicated to making a healthier and loving tomorrow for
you all.

TABLE OF CONTENTS

Chapter 1

911 May I Help You _____ 1

Chapter 2

What is The Emergency? _____ 12

Chapter 3

Making The Report: Anonymous Pink _____ 22

Chapter 4

Making The Report: Anonymous Red _____ 29

Chapter 5

Making The Report: Anonymous Green _____ 37

Chapter 6

Making The Report: Anonymous Blue _____ 42

Chapter 7

Making The Report: Anonymous Purple _____ 49

Chapter 8

Making The Report: Anonymous Brown _____ 58

Chapter 9

Making The Report: Anonymous Black _____ 66

Chapter 10

Help Is On The Way _____ 74

Chapter 11

| The Trail of Evidence | 85 |

Chapter 12

| A False Report | 95 |
| **The Art of Wounds** | **101** |

CHAPTER 1

911 May I Help You

Wounds are woven into the fabric of a painful existence. And a people's existence is displayed by way of culture. What becomes repetitive for a group of people becomes a part of the culture, and it's unfortunate that trauma in black civilization is an outfit worn constantly due to the belief of a lack of a different fit.

Prior to social media, many of us believed that our experiences were unique to only ourselves and our families. "Uncle So and So — the molester — was only in our home. That drug-addicted brother stealing all of our shit only existed with us. The alcoholic dad who pulled his gun out in angry rants when under the influence only resided where we stood. And the mom who saw fit to use that extension cord when kids used their voices or didn't agree couldn't possibly be a constant in other homes. Then came social media bringing forth this new-found transparency, and boom! There it is!

All the colorful ways in which toxicity could display itself. The familiarity washed over us like ocean waves clearing the way for true sight. How uncomfortable it was/is to watch the offspring of these colorful characters take the front stage and display all that has been written for them by way of example.

Oh wow, you too? …

Believe it or not, many grew anxious about the doors to their secrets being cracked; others felt the stuffiness leave the room and began to breathe better. Understanding you're not alone can often be a relief to those standing out on a ledge. Not that one wants others to fall with, but one may need others to help them climb back in.

There's a thin line between the jump and a second thought. Most leaped on to the web, being tangled within the feelings of it all; while others rathered a remedy to untangle what was weaved by the many who were wrapped up prior.

We watched as people began to align in trauma, even making light of the many insane rituals that their homes had in common with the homes of others. The family members that did the same things — the ass whoopings that they now believed they earned, and the logic that they shared about being tied to their abusers — because, after all, they are family. Some are even becoming allies against anyone who dared to comment against the act of remaining a victim to the experience; versus using the experience to rise. A new term was born—victim shaming—which could hold weight if not as a response to healthy advice for the purpose of getting better. There was a new tagline to shield those in pain from healing, and I ask: "why would anyone want to be shielded from that?" The line was in the sand, and it became more and more interesting to see who stood where; and what else they had in common: culture!

What is culture?

What does culture have to do with this?

Culture can be defined as a way of life, a brand of sorts: activities, traditions/rituals, and ideas that tie into the identity of a people from generation to generation. And impacts an entire society. When culture is spoken of, people often focus on the arts, food, music, style etc. however, there's an entire area of focus neglected. Art, food, and music are the beauty of culture, but not all culture is feel-good music and soul food.

Just as with everything else, there are layers upon layers that, if peeled back, may reveal a not-so-pretty side. What lies beneath is often the parts we'd rather act as if: do not exist. I compare it to wallpaper: looks great, compliments the house, and draws attention, but beneath it lies black mold that, although isn't visible to the naked eye, tends to get everyone in the house deathly ill. Let's keep in mind mold often grows in the dark. Do we allow everyone to die off, or do we crack the blinds, get that wallpaper down, kill the mold and get the family back to health?

This may seem like a simple question to the healthy mind; however, I've come to understand that comfort & routine often takes precedence over what's healthy in our society but much more within black culture.

We are in a state of emergency!

As Martin Luther King once said: "Our lives begin to end the day we are silent about things that matter."

-Martin Luther King Jr.

It's time we speak up! The mentality of a people dictates the actions of a people, and those of us who are well; understand the need for what we call: "some get right!" Our Cultural norms no longer come by way of nature, and the way we have begun to nurture has defied health. We've been stripped of the village mentality, and along with that came a loss of many other things.

There's a constant conversation between us: Black culture and many others that states: black people must unite! Although this is a true statement, there are many steps in-between separation and unity, and one of those steps must be trust! Before the village comes the family. The family creates the values and principles that we walk in to allow our connections to our village. But if the starter kit is faulty, the entire structure is weak. This is what birthed "Wounded" (A system that started as a screenplay

& books series addressing the skeletons in the black closet but today has morphed into a mental and emotional health-based system created to break generational trauma).

There's a study called cultural psychology that explores how cultural practices influence and reflect the human psyche. This means there's a correlation between the culture of a people and the psyche of a people, which is very important to examine as we identify the many areas of concern. We must recognize how culture can either build or create detriment within a society. This is why I began the conversation with culture.

So many houses echo in sorrow as the one child amongst many screams in pain while the rest find comfort in the state of numbing. Her dad isn't the only alcoholic sounding alarms. Her mother is not the only one willing to beat the voice out of her. That brother isn't the only one that will steal the ground from beneath her feet if possible. And that uncle—oh, that uncle, brother, father friend—isn't the only one murdering the childhood of the many children who crosses his path. She is not alone. Although not only synonymous with black culture, I often ask myself: "Why are we so deeply in the thick of it?"

Although the slavery conversation is sickening, it must be referenced when discussing the fact that black people have been buried deep within the trauma of that experience for centuries prior to our current bloodline even being a thought. Unfortunately, that experience is also a part of black culture. With this history came habitual behaviors learned and passed down to every generation since. So when we reflect on the health of black culture, we must consider this.

The fear-based structure carried over from that past has continuously been the blueprint for how the black family unit is run. Don't get me wrong; this can be understood by way of past circumstances; however, circumstances have changed, and behaviors have not. The rules created for survival are very different from the rules needed to live a healthy life, and so this is when things become a bit confusing.

The behaviors that once protected black people during slavery: now create vulnerability in the black family unit. And the absence of trust from the outside world has aided in the lack of trust within. The black parental goal is to raise a strong male or female instead of a healthy, happy, and thriving one, which is an obvious response to fear. And fear is what has fostered mental illness among us.

Definition submission: Mental illnesses are: health conditions involving changes in emotion, thinking, behavior, or a combination of all.

With this definition laid out for you, does it put things into context?

Would you say that we are well?

Denial sits in every room, dressed as the best friend in many homes, while beneath the costume lies a dangerous enemy designed to create the same outcome as our enslaved past. The wounds we wear on our backs today come by way of our own; often by ourselves. We are now both—the slaves and the slave masters.

Although there are many areas of wounds to be addressed throughout the "Wounded" series: the generational wounds to children that will one day likely become parents is the current focus of this book. Unfortunately, there's an imbalance between who reports their experiences by way of gender; therefore, this conversation tends to be geared more toward little girls who will one day become mothers.

I am aware that childhood sexual abuse/trauma affects both boys and girls; however, the case studies on my end slant more toward little girls, and this is what actually brought "Wounded" to the surface.

Mothers design the state of the future due to our positioning in the household. As the teachers, example, and cornerstone of the family. So if we aren't well our illness infects the health of generations to come.

I am a black girl! I desire safety—the ability to be vulnerable and not victimized. I desire the freedom to choose, as this is my birthright! I desire to be valued in such a way that my village protects me with their lives. And this innate desire has been in attendance for as long as I can remember: I assume since birth! And these desires, I've come to understand, are a large ask for those who have yet to identify that these asks are the bare minimum. I am a daughter, mother to two, sister to five, and soon-to-be grandmother to four, and with that said, I decided that the skeletons within my black closet will end with me. Inspiring all other closets to release their skeletons for the purpose of gaining their own wings.

Babies are born understanding their inner God. They come, observe, test and proceed to accomplish any challenge they face without complaints. They are easily the most valuable beings on the planet. The fact that their innocence is a reflection of the limitless possibilities to come is a gift. But these valuable beings are also the most vulnerable. And the growing number of cases being revealed leads me to believe that the elders of the world are not valuing or securing the investment as we should. Abuse towards youth is alarming on all fronts, but the sexual abuse of a minor is the focus of this conversation.

Wounds are often a collective of war. Be it a war inward or outward. What we see or experience of others is a reflection of what they're experiencing within. Studies say that predators, too, have often been victimized in some way, shape, or form. And I acknowledge their war within; however, empathizing with the plight of another doesn't dissolve them of the accountability attached to their actions. When someone fires a handgun at another, we can all understand the instinct to return fire; however, if an innocent bystander gets shot in the process, the fact that this person was shot at first; will not hold much weight to the injury or loss of life caused especially if the injury or loss of life is a loved one.

We are at war! And one is either with or against. The war within exits at some point, forcing outsiders to fight! Victims are forced to fight as a form of self-defense, and everyone else must choose a side. Children should never be the enemy; however, there seems to be an unfortunate amount of caretakers joining forces with the predators while camouflaging in love-like uniforms leaving the young confused about which side they're on and what love actually is.

What is love?

Would you be able to identify it: if it was present?

Love can be defined as the correlation between feelings, words, and actions that are displayed within the reciprocation of respect, honor, loyalty, and care as a continuum. And due to the elders that we were entrusted to showing up outside of this definition, it's hard for many of us to fathom. Our spirits recognize the conflict, but our humanity doesn't want to believe that our parents didn't know how or have the capacity to love us. We'd rather decide that love hurts! This is the largest hurdle to overcome to get where we need to be. Parents need to have the courage to admit what they already truly know: "We didn't get it right.", while the children of these parents need to accept that it isn't a betrayal to the parents to admit that your spirit understood this all along. All while also empathizing with the fact that parents had experiences that created the lack that they passed down as well.

The colors of Pain: Wounded

In this piece, we will be brought into many homes. Homes of people who are a product of many unfortunate exchanges. Homes whose walls carry the secrets of many cryptic tales. Homes that housed one of the most heinous crimes of all times, childhood sexual assault! I know some may not see this as heinous. You may think: "it's tragic, but not quite heinous... Murder is heinous!" and weighing it beside murder seems a bit extreme; however, I'd beg to differ. It is a form of murder. It kills a version of a person and then forces the existing version to live that death over and over again throughout their years. There's a level of torture that can be said to surpass murder; but only a victim would know.

We will be introduced to characters who played accessories to this act both unintentionally and intentionally. Characters who hid so deeply within their own trauma that they were pulled into the quicksand of their experiences, leaving them incapable of being there for others. We will read about entire families with the ability to bury their conscience so deep that they no longer hear its call.

As you continue to read, you will experience many stories of children: now adults: who were made to feel like their vulnerability was wasted on the opposition, and that's just as unfortunate as the physical violation that they had to experience.

I am a product of childhood sexual assault. Throughout my entire life, I've worked through my trauma via art. My life has been dedicated to pouring my feelings into my creative space through various works (fine art, visual art, music etc.) for the purpose of using all of the ugly to produce something beautiful. Art has been a form of meditation and therapy for me. But as of 2019, it became less about me and more about exploring how to serve others. I was struck by an overwhelming urge to do more. As a natural activist with a huge passion for life, I needed to zero in, mute the noise and gain a full understanding of where my passion and purpose align, as well as; what medium would be most effective in its success. And I was spiritually inspired to write a screenplay, soundtrack, and this book.

The pain I observe in the world has shown to be way too large to be packed behind a door, stacked with the bones of many, waiting to collapse with just a wiggle of the knob. So although many seem to be trying to remedy the areas of concern, I have concluded that many are focused on the effects and not the cause. The closet needs to be opened, allowing all the skeletons to hit the ground in pieces revealing a puzzle to be put together from square one. We can all relate to pain, despair, and disappointment, so I understand how we can align via the commonality of those feelings; however, the cause must be the desired focus because it's founded upon information and evidence that allows for prevention and rehabilitation. The effects only allow for a Band-Aid after the fact. And the types of wounds we are discussing are too deep, too large, and too fatal to be dressed with a Band-Aid.

CHAPTER 2

What is The Emergency?

Wounds come in many forms, but when we hear the word, we usually visualize flesh wounds—wounds from injuries that happen via violent exchanges or accidents. The fact is: wounds aren't always visible. They're often only seen by eyes that take the time to look far beyond the physical. Wounds show up in action and mindset are often hidden behind triggers. For example, the young man that appears angry or overly sensitive; or maybe deals with girls in ways that mirror misogyny did not show up this way out of thin air. And the girl who appears to be withdrawn or sexually beyond her age has often been introduced to interactions that have given lessons far beyond her. Although these actions don't all equate to one answer, they equate to an answer; and our young deserve to know that they are worth us: investigating.

But before proceeding, I have to give another definition submission. Sexual assault is pretty broad. So to make the distinction between the many different types of sexual assault for clarification. I'd like to define terms:

- An act in which one intentionally sexually touches another person without that person's consent

- Coerces or physically forces a person to engage in a sexual act against their will.

- It is a form of sexual violence that includes child sexual abuse, groping

- Rape (forced vaginal, anal, oral penetration or a drug-facilitated sexual assault)

- The torture of the person in a sexual manner.

To identify an act specifically, direct terms are used, such as: molestation or rape. To molest is to: make unwanted sexual contact of some sort with a minor. While rape is to: have some type of intercourse without consent. Each word's legal definition varies depending on the state/country. However all are very much types of sexual assault.

I'd like to prepare you. Some of the content will be triggering to many. And many of the stories are graphic because they are the tales of the victims. I chose to allow their raw voice to come through for the readers to understand their plight. However, the stories will be followed by commentary and questions that help to explore the signs, triggers, mindsets, and accountability to be taken when being the caretaker of our young in a culture that needs healing.

The stories shared in this book turn victims into victors via voice. Although anonymous, the events spoken will assist in the healing and understanding of wounds unseen. Wounds that lay beyond the surface, bruising the entire makeup of those who've been victimized and the many who have experienced them. I visualize the stages of wounds going from pink to red, red to green, green to blue, then purple to brown before turning black.

I call this "The Color Of Pain."

I was young: too young to understand sex beyond the knowledge that it was something that only elders do; when I was introduced to the fact that maybe older people do it with kids too. While everyone was out doing their own thing, I stayed home with my older brother watching Video Music Box on the living room VCR until he decided he wanted to do something different. Seven years my senior—I looked up to him the entirety of my short existence—who'd know I'd be face up, staring at his chest as he played this game that didn't feel like playing at all—house. He was the dad, and I was the mom, which led to him showing me what parents do. As uncomfortable as it was, I did what he asked. And as confused as I was, I played along. Not much playing, though; it was more like an out-of-body experience: as I watched one tear spill from my eye without even being noticed by the one who created it. This was the first time I saw male parts, and they looked strange! Not to mention I didn't like the way guys smelled.

Playing house hurts! It hurt in ways that I had never experienced pain. The interesting part was that more than the bodily harm, I felt a pain that I couldn't naturally express—what was that? The pain of separation: separating spiritually from someone who I'd been tied to since birth. Still remaining in the same spaces, even carrying on conversations but where was the connection? How did this person change so drastically in my eyes? How could I no longer recognize his spirit? That moment robbed my big brother of his greatness and robbed me of my big brother. I could no longer admire the beauty which came from him because he'd now created such ugliness in my path that no matter how hard I tried: it was almost impossible to see past it. And the more the house filled with other bodies who had no knowledge of what had taken place, the more pressure I felt to be just as oblivious as them. I acted as though this experience never struck my reality—pushing it back into the abyss of my mental vortex so that life could continue as planned. But it never really does: does it? Life goes on, but the plan is never again clear. The vision of it all is blurred: smeared by the very existence of that memory that sits way back there, waiting to be addressed. Will it ever be addressed? Today the answer to this question is yes!

- Mahagony B.

The colors of Pain: Wounded

This is my story! The story that led me on the path of healing myself and hopefully successfully assisting others. I spoke of the traumatic ways in which this type of experience changes a person because I, too, have been changed. My bruising showed up in many forms, but one example is my becoming a mother to a baby girl at the age of 15. She too was the product of an exchange with an older man—another bruise.

My bruising showed up most in my skepticism. I couldn't trust the thought of my little girl attending sleepovers or being alone with men; I had to make sure that my daughters would never share my story: they'd know of it, but it would never be theirs. The bruises showed up in many other colors along the way. Anger, lack of trust! The beauty of the innocence that a child offers was no longer. Trauma is a really eerie thing. It's kinda like getting hurt in a place your parents told you not to be: so you hide the injury because you can't bear to tell the back story knowing that you didn't belong there in the first place. A burden begins to feel like your own failed creation, growing shame like mold upon your spirit. People ask why someone doesn't tell. But how many of you speak your shame to anyone that will listen?

I was an adult when I finally shared this experience with my mother—she cried! She cried not only for me, but her wounds came to the surface as I spoke my pain. She too had wounds to expose—wounds very similar to mine. This was a pivotal moment! I now had the opportunity to see my mother in her human form: a delicate version of the strong black woman she presented prior to this day. For years I had anger towards my mother for not being present enough to pick up on the signs. I also had a great deal of disappointment in the fact that I was unprotected.

It's interesting how the "strong black woman" persona is created to protect oneself, but when one really thinks about it, all it does is create a false sense of self that can't be lived up to and leaves little room for the human experience. The overcompensation that happens in the "strong black womanhood" is a part of what led to the anger I had for my mother when it was all said and done. Someone so aggressive in her response to other circumstances, so swift in her reactions, observant of everything around; left me confused as to why I didn't seem important enough for her to detect what was happening in my world. That strong black woman isn't scared, isn't gullible, and isn't to be crossed but yet, in this instance, she had a blind spot, and that blind spot was me. So I was left feeling undervalued. Of course, after finally having the conversation, I understood her differently, but this is why transparency is so important. Having the talks, expressing one's plight, and acknowledging one's emotions, changes the entire understanding, and it leaves less unseen for those coming behind us.

But guess what? I, too, was guilty of the same lack of transparency that my mother displayed. During all the years that I kept my experience to myself, I also left others unprotected. In all of my anger and disappointment for my mother, I also had a blind spot. I will never forget the time

I finally felt the urgency to release this information within me and wanted to prepare the family for the fact that I was going public. I met with my sisters over food and spoke with them about my experience. But because they too had their own experiences, their responses were sorta numb. I also met with the one responsible for me having this experience in the first place, and his response to me speaking up was, "Aww man, I just started working at the church. Things are getting good for me; you're going to blow up my life."

The audacity!

But when I spoke with my other brother, I was struck with a hard dose of accountability when he responded, "How could you not tell me? I had him around my little girls!" That was a defining moment! I was now everything I believed my mother to be. I swallowed that truth whole, almost choking on it as it went down slowly, cutting off my air. And it forced me to take a long hard look at myself and everyone else involved. I needed to do better, be better!

I thought I was doing enough directing laser focus on my children. But to understand life, love and responsibility is to understand that our responsibility goes far beyond our children but reaches out to all. That one question my brother asked me changed everything. Prior to that conversation I thought I was on path. I was a helicopter mom: overprotective, quick to react, and a severe punisher for anyone that crossed my bounds. Needless to say, I, too, went the strong black woman route while focusing directly on the safety of my kids' bodies. I guess I did what I wished was done for me. Today I know that the extreme isn't necessarily the most healthy but back then, I had only the example presented to me, so I created a template of my own, utilizing what I found helpful and tweaking what I felt was broken. Unfortunately, my template was limited as well.

While I needed my children to know that I would give my life and freedom in exchange for their safety, I didn't quite consider all of the other children that were left unguarded.

The longer I live, the more I connect with more and more people with tracks of bruising that play as their historical map. I must say until writing this book, I never fully understood why this specific topic has yet to be confronted in a real way (When I say "real," I'm speaking of this conversation being confronted with a solution in mind). But the trip that this piece of work has taken me on says: This topic needed a very special hand… and my life put all of the dots in line for that hand to be mine! Writing this has been rough. Not only the writing of my story but going through the details of others. This has taken my spirit through the fire in a painful but cleansing way. I am triggered often. Living the truth of others for the purpose of sharing a teaching moment with the world through the lens of real to life experience. At the same time, putting myself in that bedroom, with that predator, at that moment, feeling that spirit, that exchange, that disgust! It is hard! This is more than a book but a representation of demons that plague the footprint of a culture that has so many demons already.

As a culture, we are sick. Illness is in every step of our daily stride. So much so that many believe it to be normal. If we are speaking of norms in a typical way, such as what the majority of people are doing, I guess we can say that it is so... However, when I speak of these behaviors not being normal, I am speaking in terms of nature/ natural. It is normal to see someone who suffers from Schizophrenia speaking to the voices in their heads; however, schizophrenia isn't a natural state, so this symptom would not be in existence if there wasn't an illness in attendance. And many of the behaviors that we display as a culture wouldn't be present if not for an illness being in attendance. Let's be clear.

Whether via slavery, marriage, religion or culture the past has made a common practice of men indulging in adult behaviors with little girls. So much so that to some, it was a rite of passage. For my generation—Gen X—our grandmothers didn't know a life without being identified as a girl whose purpose was for the use and consumption of men. And in some cultures, that remains the case; however, The American Psychiatric Association has seen fit to label pedophilia a mental disorder since 1968, which displays the fact that just because something is a common practice; doesn't make it healthy and doesn't make it right.

We all know the saying: "Hurt people: hurt people." So we understand that the ill will cause illness to others at some point. And this book is a representation of just that. I'm in agreement that those with the capacity to carry out sexual assault of any kind have a mental condition: or as we say it in black culture: "have a screw loose" or "are touched." But once we are aware that someone is ill, we acknowledge that they are incapable of controlling the symptoms attached to their illness which relieves a predator of their responsibility; while enforcing the need for everyone else to take on more responsibility in the matter. Therefore it is so…

CHAPTER 3

Making The Report: Anonymous Pink

PINK represents the inflamed stage of a wound. Inflammation refers to your body's process of fighting against things that harm it

Anonymous Pink,

This is the very first time I'm taking myself back to this period of my life, and it's a bit nerve-racking. It's been 30 years, but it sits right here on my chest. When I was 10yrs old, my uncle Lester was the guy who took me around with him, so I didn't feel left out not having a father and all. He played the role of my dad because my dad wasn't around. He split before I ever had the chance to know him, so it isn't much of a surprise that I craved male attention.

Some may say I was fast because I catered to the male in a room or hung on their every word, but I was just a little girl searching for my father in every male exchange that crossed my path. It often ended pretty innocently; however, other times, it ended with my mom or aunts sending me out of the room while labeling me a "fast ass" girl that needs to stay out of grown folks' faces.

On this day, I couldn't have predicted the ending. A friend of my uncle welcomed the attention and offered it right back—this was new. He was fixing a car and once he noticed I was interested, he invited me to help. I was ecstatic! This is the type of thing I always imagined dads doing with their kids. I couldn't possibly have known that I was being groomed. From that day forth, he played car guessing games with me and invited me to help him, still very innocent—that is, until he began complimenting my looks, giving me little gifts, and asking that I'd keep little secrets. I loved the compliments; they made me feel special.

I kept the secrets. It felt like we had shared something and my uncle never saw anything wrong with the exchange he was privy to, so it had to be okay. This friendship felt good. He never shunned me, called me fast for wanting to talk, or acted like it was wrong to want attention. He was my favorite person at the time.

The friendship lasted until the day my uncle took a store run leaving me with him, and our friendship took a turn.

He asked me to touch him in his private area, and I did. He made a game of making it grow in my hand, which I found funny. He asked if I had ever seen one before—I hadn't. Then he asked if I wanted to see—I did. Now some may be thinking—that's why her mom and aunts were calling her fast but someone logical would say I was curious. I was a ten-year-old child being cleverly groomed by what I viewed as a father figure. This game made me curious. I wanted to see what was growing in his pants. What does it look like? How does that happen? So I still hadn't a clue that anything that was happening was wrong. His voice was nice, and he smiled as we played. There were no signs that this was bad until he told me that mine was different but can grow too. He asked if I wanted to see and I said yes, although I wasn't quite sure what I was consenting to.

When he put his hand down my pants, my feelings changed. This part my mom did talk to me about. I reflected back to the conversation that mom and I had about no man touching me down there, and I was confused. Mom said that being touched down there was wrong... but he was nice to me. He had been my friend, and he asked if I wanted it, so if it was wrong, it wouldn't be his fault, it would be mine, right? I asked for it, so if I told, I'd be the one in trouble. This was the beginning of me keeping secrets that ate at my insides until I had nothing left.

-Anonymous Pink

The story of Anonymous Pink is interesting. A ten-year-old girl falling victim to a predator due to lacking her father's presence. This was articulated so eloquently. Having the hindsight to identify the reasoning behind her need for male attention as well as the ability to see her mom and aunties' blind spots: it feels so familiar. I can't speak for the homes of cultures outside of mine, but the black family often reacts to the effect without researching the cause. Many young victims are or were labeled fast asses. Ask yourself, have you ever come to such a conclusion? And if so, did you take the time to check for bruises?

When I first began to read this insert, Anonymous led with her uncle taking her around with him: I instantly thought her uncle was going to be the predator: which is a showing of my bruising: but Uncle Lester was a good guy, picking up where her father left off. The problem was he had a blind spot with his "friend". He must've trusted him to leave her with him, even if for a short while. Uncle Lester obviously didn't have the wounds left behind to create the necessary skepticism that my experiences have awarded me. Unfortunately, I'm sure he does now. I wish I knew how this story ended. Did Anonymous ever tell her uncle? Did the family find out years later and get their own justice? Did they let bygones be bygones? Or did they get the law involve? I guess I'll never know; however, I hope that whatever the response, he was never afforded the opportunity to strike again.

Anonymous Pink pointed out a very important detail as she spoke of being groomed.

(Grooming: The process of a child sexual offender drawing a child in by gaining his or her trust in order to sexually abuse the child and maintain secrecy. The offender may also groom the parents by persuading them of his or her trustworthiness with children).

Research says that the grooming stages go something like this: Find a victim, Gain trust, Help the victim in some way, Isolate the victim, Sexualize the relationship and finally: Maintain the relationship and power.

Therefore these offenders are labeled predators because, like a predator, they prey on and exploit others for their own consumption.

Anonymous Pink's first bruise came by way of her dad leaving, which led to her being taken advantage of sexually by another male figure. And believe it or not, there's bruising from the name-calling coming from mom and auntie. One thing that needs to be considered is the message that comes by way of labeling children fast. A little girl should not be held responsible for the actions and thoughts of men. And that specific label gives that young girl the impression that if someone does see her in a sexual way, it's not only her fault, but she's deserving of what she receives after the fact, which is absolutely not the case! And likely one of the reasons girls don't speak up sooner.

In this story, the grooming process is clear. This guy pays attention to the lack of a dad in Anonymous's life, and that's likely why he chose her. Then he gained her trust and helped her by doing what no one else was: giving her time and attention, and allowing her to be herself freely. And the isolation came by way of Uncle Lester trusting that he could leave her with him. Checkmate!

The other critical detail to acknowledge is the fact that the family did the rest of the work for him. Don't get me wrong; I understand it was unintentional; however, it must be addressed. Mom did well having a conversation with Anonymous Pink, but she gave her the cliff note version. Anonymous said:

"Mom said that being touched down there is wrong, he asked if I wanted it, so if it was wrong, it wouldn't be his fault; it would be mine…

It's very important that we find a way to become more comfortable with explaining sexual feelings and actions so that we can fully express them through detailed discussions that allow for questions, answers, and comfort for the children as well. Children will not find comfort in discussing things with us that they can clearly see are uncomfortable for us. It starts with us identifying our thought process around sex. Many girls were raised to believe that sex is bad, inappropriate, and nasty. And this understanding was passed down via parents who feared the outcome of us having early sexual experiences. And look what that caused... early sexual experiences! We didn't all have early consensual experiences, but an in-depth conversation may have protected us from those non-consensual experiences as well. The lack of information is dangerous! But on that same note, those on the outside looking in, and seeing the lack of foundation within the home, amongst the family, is dangerous too.

The mindset of the family also took part in doing the predator's work for him. Knowing that the women of the house deemed Anonymous as fast could have led to the predator's interest, as well as the thought that she wouldn't be believed if she spoke her truth. But that's just a theory. What we know for sure is that this mindset definitely led to anonymous not speaking up because she said: "I asked for it, so if I tell, I'd be the one in trouble."

Children need to know emphatically that as a child, they cannot grant permission to their bodies, and therefore, there is no situation in which they will be held responsible when it comes to a sexual act being carried out by an elder.

Families must focus on the triple C's: Community, communication, and caution because this will safeguard the family as a unit against predators.

CHAPTER 4

Making The Report: Anonymous Red

RED represents aggravation

A bruise going from pink to red is symbolic of inflammation turning into aggravation: therefore, still a very fresh wound.

The colors of Pain: Wounded

Anonymous Red,

I went to my grandmother's house for a weekend. She hosted a card game, so she was busy entertaining a company. Of the company, I was the oldest of four kids. Before the night ended, a few people were preparing to go and of the people leaving; was one of the kids I was playing with, who happened to be my grandma's close friend's son, who lived right down the block. The great part about where he lived was the fact that his complex was connected to an outdoor park that was only open to the residents. So, of course, we saw it as an opportunity to get more play time, so all of the kids asked if we could go with him until the card game was over.

When he said yes, we celebrated by jumping for joy. We got there and immediately headed to the park to play. But I needed a bathroom run, so I went inside. The bathroom was located on the main floor (same level as the park) next to his kitchen. After using the bathroom, I looked around, intrigued by how weird the layout was. I guess the curiosity of an 8yr old is what put me in harm's way. When grandma's friend saw me looking around, he said: "come here; I'd like to show you something." So he proceeded to walk me down the steps, only to see his bedroom at the bottom. He asked me what I thought about his room. I'm not sure what I was supposed to be thinking, but my thought was getting back to the park. He told me to lay down on his bed, and since grandma told us all that, we better listen, or we wouldn't be able to come back to the park, I did what I was told. As I lay there, he started fondling my chest, which is weird to think of now, knowing that I hadn't developed anything yet. He then went down my pants with his hands. I don't quite remember what my thoughts were at the moment. I know everything seemed to progress really quickly. He removed the bottom layer of my clothing — pants, underwear…and started touching himself as he touched me. I was lying there watching his penis grow bigger and bigger. He put his finger inside me, and I remember the pain throbbing throughout my body. I started to cry, but he continued without a care, in fact, he escalated. He got on top of me, trying to put his penis inside of me, but it wouldn't go. He tried a couple more times, and all I could do was yell: OUCH! OUCH! I was a fragile little girl with a grown man trying to force himself into my small space, and it hurt like hell!

I remember smelling this stench of maybe a bad cologne or something coming from his chest while he was on top of me. The amount of sweat falling from his body to mine was disgusting. He then asked me to sit up then proceeded to put himself in my mouth. It wouldn't fit there, either. He held a part of my mouth open so he could force it and ended up ripping the corners of my mouth. I gagged and cried the entire time. One of the other kids came into the house and kept calling my name. Only then did he get up and tell me to get dressed. We left to go right back to my grandmother's house. I told her what had happened, but she didn't believe me. Even when I was able to describe his place, she still didn't believe me. My aunt said she believed me because, after all, how would I know where his bedroom was located or what it looked like, but since no one took any action, I left it alone and never said anything else about it. I'm reminded daily when I look in the mirror at the scarring at the corners of my mouth.

The most disgusting part of my story is that although this was the first time I'd come in contact with a man who believed me to be there for his own consumption, it was not the last. I'm not sure what these men saw in me or why they chose me at all, but I met a similar fate when I went away for sleep away camp.

Every year I attended a sleep away camp. I usually went away for about a week, but this time I was staying for two weeks. The bus ride was about 8/9 hours from home. It felt like we would never get there. I couldn't wait to arrive so I could finally relax.

I was excited to meet everyone I would be staying with, so when we arrived, and the chaperone introduced everyone to the families they'd be staying with, I was over the moon. The lady and daughter that picked me up were nice. I looked forward to my stay. When we got to the house, the mom showed me which room I would be staying in, and I started to unpack my belongings while they started dinner. I heard a male's voice and thought: "that must be the father," as I continued unpacking my clothes.

Though I couldn't make out what he was saying—he was loud. When the door slammed, I turned around, and the dad was there. It was weird because I didn't even hear him come up the stairs. I said "hi", but he shoved me onto the bed. That was the very last thing I remembered happening. The next thing I knew, the chaperone was there. All my stuff was packed and downstairs waiting for me; my vaginal area was sore, my legs were shaking, and I was walking down the steps to leave. I walked past the mom and daughter as tears fell from their eyes. I noticed the mom had a mark on her face that wasn't there when she picked me up. She told the chaperone that they had changed their minds about me staying. So the chaperone took me with no questions asked.

I ended up staying with her for the duration of my 2 weeks. The fact that my body was violated again was baffling. I never spoke about what happened in that house, and the chaperone never mentioned anything to my parents about me staying with her. I lost an entire moment in my life that I'm sure probably doesn't want to be found. I'm still in disbelief that this would happen twice to one little girl: who is now a woman with very deep wounds.

Anonymous Red

I had to take a moment to write this response. This graphic display of horror triggered me thoroughly. And the fact that this story ends with Anonymous Red having the courage to speak up, yet is met with disbelief: grinds my gears. It's so unfortunate that there are so many stories of sexual assault that are met with this type of skepticism and denial. Where would a child find such a detailed account of events unless exposed to them? How does an eight-year-old come to the adults in their lives with a traumatic story such as this and get no follow-up? This child was: failed! It was as simple as asking the other children about their playtime with Anonymous Red to come to the conclusion that she was absent for at least a period of time: which would ultimately lead to the question: where was she during that time?

I want to be clear that I understand not 100% of claims are found credible however, all claims should be investigated. An area of concern jumped out at me in regard to the importance of clear communication when Anonymous Red speaks of doing what she was told: " since grandma told us all that we better listen or we wouldn't be able to come back to the park: I did what I was told". So many of us make this exact statement to our children but never think of the fact that children are very literal and need full statements, not partials. Not everything an adult tells a child to do is correct, so we must give context to such statements. And although we want our children to respect the chain of command, we must know that we can't give our children the understanding that all adults have earned the right to be trusted blindly. There are so many areas of bruising here!

Anonymous Red was not only sexually assaulted, but she was violently raped. The vivid way in which she painted this picture put me directly inside this room. I felt her innocence as she walked down the steps. I felt her obedience as she laid down — as told. I felt her fear and pain as she described the exchange and then felt her confusion and despair when she wasn't believed. These are all moments of bruising growing from one color to the next, deepening in soreness.

I wish I had a bit more background on grandma's friend to understand how he concluded that he could get away with this; however, being a close friend of the grandmother says that he knows her enough to somehow know that she wouldn't believe or follow up on the allegation.

I was baffled when realizing that this story wasn't the end! The first story was so heavy I couldn't stand the thought of another…but there it was! This child was brought into a situation that was supposed to be a highlight to the array of childhood memories that she stored but instead, she gained another real-life nightmare to replay in her mind for a lifetime. This is yet another scenario where not only a system failed, but all of the adults were negligent as well.

Am I to believe that sleep away camps aren't doing deep background and home checks when placing children for any amount of time? I'm floored! Not to mention the lack of questioning on the part of the chaperone: is beyond me! It's one thing to quickly take the child out of an environment that appears to have been an error, but to not ask the child if she's okay or what her experience was; especially after seeing the mother of the house wearing bruises, is unbelievable! Oh, and I mustn't forget the fact that she neglected to make the family privy to the change of plans…so much to unpack here.

The bruise in this story that sticks out the most is the fact that Anonymous Red has lost some of her memories. When someone is wounded deeply in any way the brain has a way of protecting them by taking away the thoughts, visions, and recollections of experiences that they are yet capable of confronting. It's like her bruise didn't go through the many colorful stages but went directly to the black. How does a little girl with this experience grow to be a woman that can trust anyone? How does a child with this history have harmony within a family that did not protect, believe or secure her in any way? These are the type of wounds we are dealing with from generation to generation, and we are just now having this very real conversation: it's alarming! One thing that stayed with me from my discussions with Anonymous Red was the fact that we spoke of a toxic relationship she indulged in, and when I asked: "why did you fight so hard to hold on to a relationship that wasn't good to or for you?" her reply was: "he was the first person I gave myself to willingly." And all I could think was, wow!

CHAPTER 5

Making The Report: Anonymous Green

Green is symbolic of lack of life and stagnation. It can also communicate decay. When a bruise goes from red to green it's the state of numbing.

Anonymous Green,

I was sexually abused by my next-door neighbor. My story is a bit different because he didn't touch my private parts, but it was just as damaging. This guy was bolder than most, and I myself was overcome by his audacity. He was an island man—Jamaican, I believe. He was very funny, so his humor had a way of making those around him feel safe—me included. I enjoyed it when he came around because he made me laugh. I played with his kids—in the hallway mostly—because my mom didn't want us in people's homes. To think of it, I'm guessing she was trying to protect us from people like him all along, but guys like this have a way of creating opportunities for what they want.

On this particular day, his children and I were playing in the hall, which we often did, but usually, the apartment doors stayed open for some reason, but on this day, they were closed. In the summer, the apartment doors would remain wide open to create a draft throughout the house and allow our parents to listen out for us, but on this day, it was different. Anyway, his daughters were called to their home by their mom, and they left, saying they'd be right back. I continued to play as he seemed to be doing something, going back and forth from his home to mine. After a few back-and-forths, he stayed in the hallway with me, cracking jokes and talking. There are parts of what happened that escaped me. I guess the trauma of it all left me with a few blank spots, but I remember parts. I remember him putting my hands on him and feeling this strong energy. That's what stuck with me—the energy. I felt guilty for a long time because this energy exchange brought me in as if I, too, wanted what was happening, but I didn't! I didn't even fully understand it. I remember him bringing my head to his genitals as if desiring fellatio, but he stopped pulling my head when I was close just to show me himself. This happened right in the middle of the hallway. His hands gripped mine, moving me back and forth until completing his mission, and I was just left in a state of shock. I sat in silence as he thanked me and told me how good I made him feel before going inside to clean up. I don't even remember going back into my house. I sat stuck for a while in the hall, scared by the mere fact of being so vulnerable and accessible to such an exchange. It was shocking, it was confusing, and depleting. It made me feel horrible about myself. I'm not sure what creates this self-blame besides the fact that I wasn't courageous enough to say, "No! Stop!" But I was never the same. The old me never left that project hallway. The new me entered my home as less than the person that I was when I went out to play. But there was a silver lining: years later, I found out that he had died of aids: if it had gone any further, if there would have been a fluid exchange, I could have had the same fate. But God is good, and I carry this thought with me every single day.

- Anonymous Green

The story of Anonymous Green is another jaw-dropping account of events to be discussed in detail. Although we take into account so many outcomes when speaking of childhood sexual abuse/assault, the ending to the story of Anonymous Green brought another layer to the surface. Before digging deep, I want to address the threat of STDs being transmitted in such an exchange. This is something I don't think is spoken of often; however, it is a very real thing; and another bruise on the flesh of a victim's existence.

Anonymous Green was fortunate not to have contracted the illness, but not all young people are. It's obvious that Anonymous had a level of bruising before the encounter, a bruising that was only visible via her lack of trust and communication in her parents but that bruise became darker the moment the guy who always made her laugh became the reason her smile was hard to come by.

It's important to identify a pattern already forming. The charismatic individual already close or within the family that comes across as trustworthy due to their ability to charm those around is to be paid attention to. Let's be clear not all who are likeable are predators or people looking for a loophole within a household to infiltrate, but one mustn't keep them in the range of a blind spot because they appear cool, fun, or funny.

This piece is in no way created for the purpose of acting in fear; however, it is created for the purpose of making one aware and present within their relationships.

Something that is once again glaring in these stories is the lack of trust, communication, and comfort within the family construct, which is needed for young people to be forthcoming with their experiences. As said prior; although there are many reasons that victims don't speak up when such violations come into their lives, a huge part of the solution must be maintaining the triple C's so that young people are willing to come forth and their predators cannot continue their spree of violence.

Another thing that stood out was the guilt that Anonymous Green spoke of. Being a child who finds themselves in a situation that they can't control feeling feelings that they cannot control is also a huge part of the trauma. We have no control over what arouses us, and because of this, the guilt of feeling aroused in a situation that we acknowledge as inappropriate and unwanted absolutely bruises and creates self-blame in victims pretty often. I thought this was a great point to be addressed.

In this story, it's very reasonable to believe that this man has gotten away with this plenty prior to this particular situation. That level of audacity doesn't come by way of being a first-timer: the fact that anonymous Green spoke of playing with his daughters leads me to believe that some of his other victims may have been living right within his home. Very similar to the story prior, Anonymous Green has deleted parts of this memory for her own sanity. There are so many people who feel the residue of the trauma they've been through without having a full recollection of the experience but the bruises definitely show up in their relationships and their triggers out in the world.

CHAPTER 6

Making The Report: Anonymous Blue

Blue represents distraught. Going from green to blue is symbolic of numbness wearing off and pain coming through.

The colors of Pain: Wounded

Anonymous Blue,

I didn't find out until late that I was not the only one sexually assaulted, but so were my two sisters, a few acquaintances, and a cousin—all by the same man (my cousin's dad). Let that sink in. I seemed to be the only one in the dark, which left me completely unguarded. I trusted him. I mean, he is my uncle, the brother of my dad, and highly respected in the world. He ran his own schools, so he was around kids regularly. So excited about meeting new friends, I jumped at the chance to go to work with him.

The early portion of the day was great. The girls embraced me, some of the boys catered to me, and we played games and did a science experiment that I couldn't wait to get home to share with my mom, but at the end of the day, it got a bit different. After dismissal, my uncle said he had a few things to do before leaving so we stayed behind.

I kept catching him staring at me. The first couple of times, he'd look away as soon as I turned towards him, but after a while, I guess he decided he would let me know that he was staring, so we had a stare down before I laughed and asked, "Why are you looking at me like that?" He laughed, "Like what? Eyes are made for looking, aren't they?" I replied, "I guess." He started asking me questions about dating. Have I started? Am I still a virgin? I was weirded out about the questioning, but he knew how to frame it so that I'd become a little bit comfortable, and I did. So I told him about a boy I liked, and the dialogue changed. I was thrown completely off.

My uncle asked, "Do you know how to please a boy?" "What?" I asked. He said, "I mean, boys and girls like different things. Do you know what boys like?" In my mind, I said, "oh, I was tripping." I thought he was saying something else. But out loud, I said, "you mean how girls like compliments and boys like us to watch them show off? Yes, I know!"

"Okay, you know a little something, but I'm talking about touches. What makes a guy feel good."

"Eew!" I said. He responded: "It's not 'eew' if you think it's 'eew' you're not ready for a boyfriend."

At this point I'm twelve years old, about to be thirteen. I'm well aware of what is and isn't appropriate, and to this day, I'm still confused as to why he tried me because I am not timid like my sisters, but I guess he saw a challenge in me or something.

I wasn't sure where he was going with the conversation, so I allowed him to reveal it.

"Let me show you something," he said "close your eyes."

So I did. In my mind, I thought that my uncle was playing some dumb game with me, but when I felt him getting close, I began to peek, but I couldn't see much because he was too close to see anything. When I hear heavy breathing, I open my eyes completely and see my uncle in front of me, holding himself in his hands and masturbating right in front of me. I pushed him away from me and ran. When I got outside, I called my mom trying to tell her I needed her to come to get me and explained what my uncle did. It was a very uncomfortable conversation that confused me even more.

Not only did she not seem surprised, she continued to act as if she didn't really grasp what I was telling her, but it was very simple I told her exactly what happened. When I got home after a cab ride that felt like forever, my mom proceeded to sit me down and explain that my uncle was sick. I was blown away: not only did she allow me to spend alone time with this "sick" man, but I didn't see the response I would expect from a parent who had just gotten the news she received. This day not only changed the relationship between my uncle and I, but my mother and I were never the same again.

- Anonymous Blue

The story of Anonymous Blue is just as tragic as the rest, but her ability to confront this violation head-on was a breath of fresh air, although the response wasn't a favorable one. It was interesting to read that even Anonymous Blue had an idea of what a predator looks for in a victim, as she described: "I'm still confused as to why he tried me, because I am not timid like my sisters, but I guess he saw a challenge in me or something." The fact that anonymous identified a timid personality as victim-like is a very popular thought; however, predators are driven by the need for power, so both timid personalities and challenging personalities create a space for enforcing dominance and receiving the dose of the power trip that a predator craves.

Because Anonymous isn't the typical passive personality, her uncle needed to find a lane for vulnerability, and a teenager in the pubescent stage intrigued by boys, he sought out as her area of weakness. I'm just happy that her antenna went up. You would be surprised how many sick older males are watching young girls and their crushes, thinking about how much more they can provide or show them as if in competition with these young people. The fact that her uncle utilized her interest in boys to manipulate her into a sexual act was definitely wild.

Anonymous described her uncle as highly regarded, which is a common thing among predators. Working in schools or volunteering around children is something that is also known as a pattern for those looking to prey on the young. It's problematic that Anonymous was able to run down quite a few victims but wasn't made privy to the information until she was victimized. I know that many were raised with concepts such as not airing the family's dirty laundry, and children shouldn't be burdened with adult issues, as well as the thought that privacy is equivalent to secretiveness; however, this practice is exactly what makes an entire family vulnerable. It creates a culture of attracting exactly what is supposedly trying to be prevented. Although this story cannot be categorized as molestation, it is absolutely sexual abuse and could have become molestation or rape had Anonymous's uncle had his way.

I added this particular story for the purpose of identifying the levels of sexual assault as well as highlighting the many markers that showed up as a result of this predatory act. Some may not see the severity in this story due to a full encounter not being carried out or due to the fact that she hadn't been touched physically, but the depth of a wound is usually identified by the mental, emotional and spiritual toll it takes on a victim.

The trust that no longer exists within a person after an experience. The guard is now positioned among the entire world because one no longer knows what to expect. The PTSD that infringes on one's ability to decipher between people who truly care for them versus people who are looking for their opportunity to pounce. The psychology of such an experience is so much larger than the semantics.

This story presented the dynamics of many black households that I continue to speak of in regard to family secrets and lack of accountability when it comes to these secrets—creating a trail of bruising that wound an entire legacy. Unfortunately, Anonymous Blue's mom dropped the ball multiple times and she will now have to take responsibility for the bruising of many wounded victims, although her guilt has likely brought upon some heavy bruising of its own. The women of the house turning a blind eye to such exchanges bring forth questions of their backgrounds, what have their experiences been? I've found that the blind eye often comes by way of their bruising. This is often the display of someone who has also encountered the experience but still has yet to find the strength or willingness to confront it. So much to unpack!

CHAPTER 7

Making The Report: Anonymous Purple

Purple represents disdain. The process of transitioning from blue to purple is less physical and more mental and emotional, really dealing with the understanding that you are bruised and how that bruising presents itself in your life.

Anonymous Purple,

I was the perfect target! A young girl on a pedestal amongst the family with a body that developed way before its time, not to mention growing up as the only child in my home. I was a straight-A student, never got into trouble, and was very introverted. It was the perfect packaging to everyone else, but I yearned for community. Luckily I didn't have to go that far because I had three cool older cousins (5-8yrs my senior). I loved my cousins, but they were the exact opposite; having essentially no structure at home, running wild and free; plus we weren't peers, so my dad hardly ever let me hang out with them. That was unless the entire family was gathering, and still then, I only got to spend the night if there were no other options.

The relationship between the 4 of us was not traditional because the relationship between our parents, who were siblings, wasn't the greatest, so the separation and lack of connection that I was trying to compensate for; weren't being met. Being heavily referred to as the "perfect child" by both my father and grandmother didn't help. So there was this unspoken energy around me that I didn't completely understand back then; however, it's all very clear today. I stayed with my grandmother for a couple of years, and since she was my older male cousin's caretaker, it also meant I shared a home with him.

We would be left home alone on certain bible study days or when dad had to work a little late: and since he's older, he would be in charge.

One afternoon school let out for a half day, so we were home early. Grandma made sure she laid down the rules before leaving. She would always say, "He's the oldest, so if he asks you to do something, don't give him no lip! But you're smart; you know right from wrong." I never really understood why I was the only one who got rules when I never got into trouble, but my cousin, on the other hand, was the problem child and was in charge. It didn't make much sense, but it's how it was so…

Our norm was clean up, he fixed us food, and I did my homework. Up until this day, things were okay. I mean, there were weird glances or sly jokes, "accidental" brushes against me in the hall, and play fighting that would sometimes get a little rough, but upon mentioning it, I was made to feel like this was normal behavior, so no real alarms went off. It kinda fell on deaf ears.

I was definitely not prepared for the escalation, though. I remember going to let the futon down in the living room so that we could lay across it on opposite ends (as dad always suggested) while my cousin was rummaging through dad's movie collection, finding something for us to watch.

By the time I'd finally got done struggling with the futon, he said he had 2 options for us while holding the movies behind his back. When he revealed them, I knew something was off and immediately got nervous because even though they weren't in my possession, I didn't want to get caught. He had one of dad's "private stash" videos

The colors of Pain: Wounded

in the blank black case and a movie called Original Sin (released in 2001...it's 2022, and I'm 28...you do the math). I didn't really know what they were about, but I knew dad never let me watch them, so that was enough to know we shouldn't be touching it, and I told him that.

He had this weird grin on his face that made me uncomfortable, so I said I had to go to the bathroom and took off toward the back of the apartment. My intention was to text my dad, but I had left the room so fast that I didn't realize I had left my phone until it was too late. A few minutes went by, and I never heard the TV, so I assumed he was waiting for me to come back out before he put the movie on, but as I exited the bathroom, he jumped out from around the corner, pushing onto me, scaring me half to death which landed me in grandma's room beside her bed. I said, "You play too much." He reached his hand out laughing, and I grabbed it, thinking he was trying to help, but the way he pulled me up forced me right into him; I hadn't a clue what he was up to, but I didn't feel right, so I went for the door only to be flung on my grandmother's bed face down putting his weight on top of me. I can still feel his hot, stink breath on the back of my neck while his hands roamed my young body as I fought to get him off of me to no avail.

His left hand slid into my pajama pants, followed by my favorite panties with watermelons and cherries on them. I picked them out myself. Now he has picked me to be at his mercy. He struggled to get between my body and the bed then fought to pry my legs open. I folded my legs closed like when you have to use the bathroom, but… have to hold it. With him being older and larger, he succeeded in wearing me thin and began rubbing his body against mine, his breaths got heavier, and his ashy skinny fingers rubbed me until the friction hurt so bad I cried. The weight of his body was crushing me. I struggled for air, and although the rubbing of his fingers hurt, they never went any further than that.

He had something worse in mind. He pulled my pants and underwear down just under my butt, licked his fingers, and rubbed them between my cheeks a few times, preparing me for entry. I wanted my dad to come home early so badly! Or at least for grandma to have forgotten something but no one ever came. He told me, "just relax and open up; remember what grandma said…I know you've been wanting this." At this point, I blacked out, closing my eyes shut as tight as I could. He held my hand as he grabbed his penis and proceeded to try repeatedly to enter where only things should exit. It was the most excruciating pain I've ever felt in my short life, and I just wanted it to stop, but it didn't.

He was satisfied just getting the head in, and he pumped on top of me for what seemed like hours but was probably only a few minutes. The next thing I remembered was him getting off of me and going back into the living room as if nothing happened; while I was left hanging off the side of the bed weak, feeling defeated, alone, dead. I don't know how long I was there, and I don't remember cleaning myself up or anything. I just knew that by the time grandma got home, I was lying on that futon where I was supposed to be. Perfection didn't protect me. Following the rules didn't protect me. I never said anything because they hadn't responded to complaints prior, so I just knew they wouldn't believe me now. When they asked what was wrong, he told them that I was struggling to use the bathroom earlier in the day, which is why I couldn't sit on my butt with my feet tucked under me comfortably like I was known for doing.

I was never the same after that. Needless to say, this abuse didn't stop there until his mom regained custody of him, and we no longer lived in the same home; it just became less frequent only when he was visiting. I did, however, come to find out later in life that he was doing the same thing with my other 2 girl cousins. I found out at a sleepover one night, but the difference was they were in the same age bracket and enjoyed it. It was obvious they messed with each other like this regularly.

That was also the night that my abuser went from 1 to 3. I became the new toy everyone made sure to play with now that they knew he opened me up, and this went on for years.

When I was 15, I overheard my aunts and grandmother talking in reference to him and his tendencies, but each defending it with the excuse, "we know he's not wrapped too tight" I was baffled because it's like they knew his potential and did nothing to keep me safe especially considering they all have been victims of sexual violation at the hands of family members when they were young. Still, to this day, I can't wrap my mind around the slackness of it all…and they all went on to lead seemingly normal lives.

Anonymous Purple

This is yet another story that was hard to read. I was there with Anonymous Purple in her horror! I must be honest and say the more stories of young ladies who come from homes that turn a deaf ear to their trauma upsets me profusely. I cannot mention enough the importance that no stone goes left unturned when it comes to our young! Not a person exists that can give me a story about why my child can't sit on her butt without it turning into millions of questions followed by an investigation.

And the fact that he was capable of coming up with that story says so much about him and his comfort in the space of being a predator! When children complain about being dealt with roughly when children tell adults anything that doesn't feel natural to them, these complaints should be taken seriously, even if just for a conversation about what and why they're feeling what they're feeling. We shouldn't be too busy to have healthy exchanges with our children. The family unit is supposed to be the most positively impactful interaction in a child's life, but instead, many are experiencing the exact opposite.

The fact that the family knew that the cousin had some issues in this area or, as they said, "wasn't wrapped too tight," but still had no problem leaving him alone with a young girl is what's pissing me off. How many stories within black culture must have this cycle before someone decides enough is enough?!

The highlighting of generations moving forward as normal is a major part of the mental and emotional health of the black community, and understanding that this so-called "normal" isn't normal at all is why this book exists. This girl was raped! In the most heinous way and had to carry this bruise around with no outlet. As adults, many don't want to imagine their anus being messed with, so imagine the pain this child had to endure. The layers of bruising that come by way of losing your voice is dark but that voice being taken away by a predator who knows exactly how to manipulate that lack of voice is darker!

This may feel like a rant because I'm triggered! But let me be clear, I'm triggered by the disgust of how little value a child/little girl has in a culture that we are told to take pride in. I'm triggered by the cycle of abuse by way of family members while said family member is still invited to the cookout! It's disgusting! It's further abuse and everyone who has knowledge of any part must be held accountable.

This story has more layers than could be shared. As you can see at the end, Anonymous alluded to many more similar experiences by way of the other cousins. And although we aren't sharing the details with all, I'm sure you can imagine the bruising that comes from multiple victimizers and constant abuse by people she desired a healthy exchange with. I mustn't neglect to point out that she mentioned the other cousins being female. Although these types of conversations often target the male species, we mustn't forget that women can also be predators. Pay attention to the character of all whom you invite in your space.

CHAPTER 8

Making The Report: Anonymous Brown

Brown represents wounds that have stalled in the healing process, which means that the wound is not going to heal unless more aggressive care is rendered. When a wound goes from purple to brown, it's asking to be addressed because it wants to be better.

Anonymous Brown,

When I was asked to be a part of this, I had mixed emotions. This is totally needed right now, but I'm hella embarrassed. And then I had to ask myself: "where'd the embarrassment come from?" I guess I'm embarrassed by the thought of what others will think when they hear of what I did. Although I was a kid and was made to do it, I still feel disgusted when I recollect it all.

My abuser was a babysitter who was great in the beginning. I loved her, and yes, my abuser was a girl. My parents loved her too, but after a while, her behavior in front of my parents was very different from her behavior when my parents were gone. I was eight, and my parents thought it would be a good idea to have a teenage babysitter (16yrs old) because she was still youthful, playful, and fun. I liked the idea too, because she was down to play with me when others acted as if they were too busy. But the way we played changed.

At first, she played with my Barbie's with me and didn't mind sitting through my tea parties or running around the park with me. I thought she was hella cool, but then she introduced me to the fort. This was when she made a makeshift cave under the covers that were our little private playground, and that too was fun at first. But I guess when people like her know that what they're doing isn't okay, there's a process before getting right to it. When we first started playing in the fort, we talked in there with snacks and brought toys in, then we began playing make-believe, and that was cool too, but one afternoon make-believe turned into a porn instructional. At 8 years old, I'm clueless, but even children need no clue to understand when they're uncomfortable. One day in the fort, we played peek-a-boo which she turned into a game of flashing. She showed me hers, and I showed her mine. I can't lie; that part was funny, but then she went beneath my house dress and touched my cookie (for the sake of not being vulgar, we will call it that) and then asked me to touch hers. Hers was wet and smelled nasty. I touched it, but I was ready to play another game. I didn't see the fun in that one, but she wasn't ready to change the game yet. She told me to lie down and close my eyes. She was going to show me something. She licked my cookie. I was confused. It felt weird. I opened my eyes: "eww!" She responded, "Close your eyes, and let me finish." She continued, and I did start to like the feeling, but then she instructed me to do it to her, and I didn't like that. I told her I didn't want to, and she said, "didn't it feel good? That's the game, I do it to you, and you do it to me; now it's your turn." I didn't want to when I touched it: it was slimy, and I didn't want to put my mouth there. I was yucked out! But I slowly eased in to do what I was told. I licked, and I didn't like the taste, so again, I responded with an, "eww, I don't want to," she pushed my head and held me down there, telling me to lick it until she was ready to let me up. When she did, I was over her. I wanted to clean my mouth and create distance, so that's what I did. She kept finding me around the house to, I guess, try to make me feel better about it, but I didn't.

She maintained that this was our secret, so when my parents got back, I didn't say anything, but my mother noticed I was acting differently and asked if I was okay. I shook my head yes, although I wanted to say no. After the babysitter left, a few days passed before my parents said she would be coming back to watch me because they had things to do. When I responded that I didn't want to be with her my mother started asking more questions because, as I said, I liked her prior, so not wanting her around was new. After constant probing, I finally told my mom our secret, and that became a whole other situation.

I never saw my mother so angry, and my father seemed ready to risk it all, but when they involved the police, it felt like I should've kept my mouth shut. I don't know how they do things now, but back then, the police involvement felt like you were being punished. I felt happy that she wasn't coming back, but I also was bothered by the experience of how it was all handled. I guess parents are damned if they do and damned if they don't, but I now have my own kids, and I still wouldn't know the perfect way to handle such a thing.

Anonymous Brown

Anonymous Brown experienced not only a female predator but a youth predator. These cases are often very delicate due to the likeliness that if a young person has taken on this behavior it's because they were likely also a victim of this behavior. Does that clear them of responsibility? No! Because if they, too, carry on this behavior knowing enough to be secretive and hide, it shows that they have the understanding that the behavior is wrong. But we often empathize more due to the possibility of that back story.

This case made me really upset because of all of these thoughts and layers to be considered. The constant nexus creating a trail of wounded people seems to never end. To be honest, I'm torn about the ways in which to respond to this because, just as in the rest of the stories, what Anonymous Brown went through was sickening and vile, and my response must reflect this with no mercy in that regard, all while considering that although much older: this predator was a child as well. However, if we really think about it, every predator was a child at one point.

I'm happy Anonymous disclosed this encounter with her parents, but I truly would have loved to know the type of rehabilitation, if any, that took place to ensure that the babysitter did not take this behavior into adulthood. I'm also curious about how her parents handled her and her backstory once this came to light. It's interesting how intricate this gets at every stage, the power dynamic, the right vs. wrong, the victim turned predator. Is it even fair to call a child a predator? And if not, does this somehow feel like a disregard for the victim/victims of his/her spree?

When dissecting this particular story, it had a different effect on me than the rest. It forced me to look at this with very different eyes if I'm being honest. I've always had a problem with the empathy shown to predators by way of their past story because it felt like excusing what I know to be a brutal life-changing encounter; however, just like the slave conversation at the beginning of this book, its relevance has to be considered while understanding that accountability still stands. Right and wrong remain whether we can empathize with the why or not. And with that being said, I am going to take this time to present the way in which I define right from wrong.

Right and wrong are identified by way of choice. If one robs another of choice: IT'S WRONG! Some will say: Well, I know people with statutory charges from situations with girls or boys who agreed to the encounter. My response to this is: We still understand the difference between girls and women, boys and men. We understand that parents make choices for children until adulthood because they are yet equipped to make solid decisions on their own behalf. So that example wouldn't count!

How many of you would have chosen candy in the morning as children? How many of you would have chosen never to eat a veggie or take chances with just about anything that someone couldn't talk you into today? That's the difference. Youth haven't the experience or understanding of the severity of cause and effect, actions resulting in response, or what many call Karma. Adults are in place to teach, inspire and guide children through their youths to hopefully make it to adulthood without permanent or negative life-altering wounds. And this responsibility is what makes these stories so gut-wrenching.

We are failing as the protectors. And those who've appointed themselves in place to take advantage of the blind spots are the ugliest of all. But we can't close our eyes to those who protect the predator over the prey. Anonymous Brown should be applauded for telling her parents. And her parents should be applauded for paying close enough attention to pick up on the visual cues that led them to question things.

It was interesting to read that Anonymous Brown felt the police encounter was a whole other violation because I related to this as well. I had two police encounters as a child that made me feel exactly this way, and I was angry at my mother for years behind it. I know that as parents, we are doing our best and doing what we know how to do. However, we must acknowledge that as we speak of culture, there are many elements. A part of our culture is understanding our reality really early in life. And that reality doesn't make for great companionship with law enforcement.

Children who grow up understanding the police as less than trustworthy don't often feel comfortable going to them when in an already traumatizing situation. And the training that police have doesn't necessarily exude honesty because they're trained to say whatever is necessary to get their desired outcome, which does not equate to a safe space. The solution here goes back to my dialogue throughout the entire book: Transparency!

Parents should explain the process clearly, every step of the way. There needs to be dialogue preparing the child for what's next. This creates trust and comfort for the process as well as the parent-child bond.

When it comes to the actual act that took place between the babysitter and Anonymous, I believe anyone would be traumatized. Holding someone's head down, and controlling them in a position they don't want to be in is horrible all on its own! So to add the sexual component makes it that much more serious. I wonder how that experience affects Anonymous today in regard to relationships with women and romantic relationships as a whole. She was very clear that she was bruised by way of the police involvement as well as the actual act but didn't give much background on what those bruises looked like, so that was a bit of a cliffhanger as well, but I appreciate the honesty brought forth about her lack of knowledge on how she would respond if facing the same dilemma with her children.

CHAPTER 9

Making The Report: Anonymous Black

Black represents an inner death. The transition from brown to black is symbolic of the clotting of all the emotions, thoughts, and baggage that no longer has a flowing path. However, the beauty of this stage… it comes right before healing.

Anonymous Black,

I've finally built up the strength to speak about this. This is not something a man wants to experience or even admit. Unfortunately, in this society, no matter if you were placed in a situation willingly or unwillingly, people have the same response; or shall I say, black people have the same response. My life has been a shell of a life due to an experience as a child, and I'm a grown man! It's like I have PTSD. I'm not comfortable with closeness, intimacy, and natural brotherly exchanges because some man decided he could force his will on me. A man I looked up to. It's crazy how I empathize with women by way of this experience because I get it. I get how someone can feel powerless in the company of someone being so powerful. I get how someone can feel a level of importance to not disappoint another even while being disappointed. I understand doing something you're not okay with because you can't picture the other options at the moment. And I understand how someone becomes overly masculine due to having to prove that: that experience doesn't define them.

This is pouring out because I needed this outlet. I'm a black man with not a lot of safe spaces: if any. I was a young teen when I was taken advantage of and when I tried to tell someone, the response felt like I was old enough to know better, which sent me right back into hiding. So this anonymous writing piece is God-sent. As a young boy growing up in the '80s, there were crews all around me, and just like most, I wanted to be a part of it all. Hip-hop culture was growing, and the families outside of the home were growing too. I got with a group of guys who were known for break dancing, and this was a big deal. I was taken under the wing by some of the older leaders of the crew, which gave me street cred, and I loved every minute of it. We went from block to block battling and doing graffiti; that's how things were back then.

I'm from the Bronx where it all began. And if you know the history of the Bronx, you know that this is where the poor of the poor stayed. But also the most creative beings you can come across. We didn't dwell on how much we didn't have because we had unity and we had culture, so when one found their crew or, as I say, family outside of the home—it stuck. I ate and slept at home, but those memories were built outside. The part that strikes me is how much space the bad memories take up, no matter how many great memories I've downloaded.

When I stare at my ceiling at night, I'm not recollecting the laughter, jokes, and wins… I'm recollecting the losses. And I lost big! I lost a big brother and friend at the same time that I lost myself. I remember like it was yesterday going uptown on the train to meet: let's call him Trey. Trey was my big homie but more like an older brother and confidant. When I got there, Trey was with Dodge (both names are made up for the sake of anonymity). Dodge was my friend, older but closer in age than Trey. We were meeting up to practice a new routine, but for some reason, Trey wanted to take practice to his house. Dodge and I thought nothing of it, but after being there for about an hour, Trey wanted to take a break. It was cool but his break started looking different when he started getting more comfortable; shorts, T-shirt, and slippers. I asked: "Are we not practicing anymore?" he responded, "chill out; we are gonna get back to it." So we started watching kung-fu flicks waiting to get back to it when Trey switched to porn and asked if we ever saw one. I laughed because I hadn't, but I was excited to see one at that moment. Dodge didn't seem like he ever saw one before, either, but he said he did. It started with mischievous laughter about doing something we weren't supposed to, then Trey changed the video to one with guys doing stuff, and I was over it. Dodge seemed to be as well by the look on his face. We caught eyes as if agreeing that this changed things, but Trey pulled his penis out and started to play with it. I was ready to go, so I said: "Umm, if we aren't dancing anymore, I will catch y'all tomorrow." but Trey said, "don't leave, I want to show you something; why are you acting like a punk. You have one too, you don't touch it? As if I was the one being weird." Then he turned to Dodge and said: "I know you jerk yours, right?" Dodge went along with it, "Yea!" so Trey said, "go ahead, let me see; show Anonymous how it's done!" Dodge began reluctantly pulling his out as Trey turned to me and said: "you look scared, don't be. I got you!" Walked towards me and rubbed his hands across the front of my pants. I jumped back. He closed the gap and said, "We all do it, we're crew, why are you buggin? Relax!" while reaching into my sweats and grabbing mine. He called dodge over and told him: "Do me while I do him." I came for the first time ever in this man's hand and hadn't a clue what to feel. It felt like nothing I had ever felt before, like I exploded from the inside! It felt good, but it didn't feel good to my spirit, if you know what I mean. I also didn't know what to make of the entire situation. Dodge was doing him, him doing me, and no matter how much I didn't want it, my body obviously did. I was confused as to what all of this meant for me. I cleaned up, but with all the awkward looks and feelings going through the house, I just wanted out, so I told them both I was going home. Trey asked, "You're gonna keep this between us right?" I replied, "Yes" and left. And that's exactly what I did. I stopped meeting up with the crew, and anytime Dodge and I crossed paths, it was awkward. We never spoke of it. We actually never spoke of anything; we would kinda give each other the head nod and move along. Any time I ran into Trey, I just went in the opposite direction. But this moment has hindered every relationship I ever had.

Anonymous Black

I found it interesting that Anonymous Black started by speaking about the effects of his encounter versus starting with the cause. This was very different from the rest of the entries in a very powerful way. I felt him first! I had an emotional tie before the picture was even painted. I was able to empathize differently after the cause and effect became one. It definitely sheds light on why people often lead with feelings instead of the act, but it doesn't quite get to the gut of it until the details come into play.

The mere fact that this was a story from the perspective of a male victim brought on an entirely new layer that was necessary to this conversation. It was relative as someone who has also had a childhood sexual abuse experience while sensitive to the dynamics of how this could possibly affect a boy: now a man. It never ceases to amaze me how typical pedophiles are with their approach when engaging young people. It's the same old story.

As I began reading the details of his encounter, I knew what was coming before it came. The bruise that is constant in all stories, no matter the variation, is betrayal. The moment that someone you were fond of uses that connection to now capitalize negatively upon the bond is the largest emotional blow. It's like being sucker punched by a friend that you didn't even know you were quarreling with. It's that moment that your friend turns into something else, and you don't quite know what to call it. But you know it isn't good. There's an unspoken safety that we feel with those we enjoy time and space with; that wouldn't exist if we hadn't our own personal character-build of them in our heads, but at this moment, the person we believed them to be is no longer, the avatar is gone, and you're forced to see that whom you are currently experiencing is the reality—it's painful.

This child looked up to a man whom he presumed as a mentor, a family of sorts, while this man saw him as an opportunity to flex his muscle (no pun intended). To acknowledge the fact that Anonymous Black says this was his very first sexual experience is to also acknowledge how the first impression is a lasting one. "The first of" everything is monumental. But his first is now attached to his largest scar, and that would be easy for no one. A pubertal teenager is already in a state of confusion and self-identification, so the first encounter with any sexual act is mind-altering. But coming by way of an adult, a man: had to spark greater confusion. That sense of believing that one lacks control due to the power dynamic: especially as a male: and the guilt of not being assertive enough to stand your ground are bruises that can harass you for a lifetime. And we can't forget the guilt of the bruise I brought up prior: The guilt of enjoying the sensation from an act that wasn't wanted, that wasn't consented to, that brought both a level of satisfaction and erosion simultaneously. This is a wound that isn't easily healed.

Although the cries are coming from the rooftops to secure girls and women in this situation, I'm sure that we would be mortified by the number of boys and men with this experience if there were no double standards and more safe spaces for our male counterparts to speak their truth. As Anonymous Black said: "I'm a black man with not a lot of safe spaces, if any. I was a young teen when I was taken advantage of… when I tried to tell someone, the response felt like I was old enough to know better, which sent me right back into hiding."

I'm sure many men feel this way. Many are too ashamed to speak about their trauma, and many fall on the cusp of the double standard. There are many boys who have lost their virginity to women but don't acknowledge it as sexual assault. They see it as more of a badge of honor, and this too shows up as bruising as we witness hyper-sexual men, womanizers, men who are totally detached from the intimacy of a sexual exchange etc. More men are affected by those exchanges than they even realize, and we must acknowledge this as childhood sexual assault as well. Anonymous Black said: "It's like I have PTSD. I'm not comfortable with closeness, intimacy, and natural brotherly exchanges because some man decided he could force his will on me." I wonder if Anonymous Black would have the same outlook and response had his abuser been a woman…just a thought.

Be it male or female, if taking advantage of the power dynamic when dealing with children, it deserves an equal response because it is damaging regardless of how differently the damage shows up. I've spoken to many; guys who smile as they speak of what they deem to be a story of them conquering an older girl or woman, oblivious to the fact that they were actually the ones conquered while being completely blind to how prevalent it is in their current toxic state. And I often wonder, "Who would he have been had he not had this experience?" Which is the same question I ask about myself and all others whom I share this bruise with.

CHAPTER 10

Help Is On The Way

From pink I crept through the colorful stages until reaching blackness. I combed through layers of trauma. Depth of pain that only each of those sharing their stories fully understands. All while trying to paint their picture as close to their actual experience as possible. I walked through seven stories (not counting my own) wearing the shoes of each character; some fit, some hurt my feet, and others flip-flopped as they were larger than expected. Watching my step, looking around at the scene of the crime. So uncomfortable at times I tried to run through it, but those shoes made sure that I took one step at a time. Slowing my pace to ensure that I lived it all, felt it all, saw it all, and even heard and smelt it all.

I tried to experience every detail, but because I wasn't there, as close as I may come to visualizing their illustration, there are still intricacies that escape me. And if we are being fully transparent, there may be details that escaped the victims as well, details that wouldn't have been lost in the moment. This is why my will is that this conversation, this project, and the upcoming system will prevent as many from having this experience as possible, but for those who for some reason find themselves on this familiar street; My hope for them is to find the voice to narrate their story in real-time, not a moment passing, no stone left unturned because there's not a detail missing when you are in it. My will is that there will be no more cries unheard or unexamined. The elders in charge will be healthy enough to be for the young: what they wish their elders were for them.

At the very beginning of this book I said: "there are many steps in between separation and unity, and one of those steps must be trust! Although this is not the only area to examine the trust within black culture; I found it to be the most impactful as we are able to see the layers of betrayal starting at such a young age, putting dots together when it comes to the family dynamic and all the moments that fracture the trust in the first place. The parents, grandparents, aunties, and uncles that failed to respond in a way that could keep the foundation of trust intact. We've heard in just these few cases, family members who ignored bruises while blaming the child, "Fast ass!"

We've heard parents that completely neglected to hear cries while being told directly that something has gone on:

"I told her what happened, but she didn't believe me. Even when I was able to describe his place, she still didn't believe me."

We've heard of an auntie that said she actually believed the child but made nothing of it:

"My aunt said she believed me because, after all: how would I know where his bedroom was located or what it looked like…"

And we have heard children respond with silence after concluding that their voice wouldn't be loud enough to pierce through deaf ears.

"But since no one took any action, I left it alone."

How must one feel when the actions of loved ones send the message that love doesn't live there at all? How must one cope with the understanding that they are dying within but must hold up appearances for the people who appear to be family but have now been revealed as mere relatives?

The most important part of life is the principles from which we pull. As a people, our intrinsic value displays itself within the principles we live by; therefore, our principles are our foundation. And that foundation decides the stability of all that is built upon it. With that said, the same goes for family and culture. Trust is a major part of our foundation and is a byproduct of a principle called integrity. And the moment that any of us witness a lack of integrity, we lose trust no matter what level of life we are in. So to experience the adults in our immediate world, who we've grown to love, believe ourselves to know, and often admire, showing up with a lack of integrity changes the entire world as we know it. Innocence dissolves the moment a child finds themselves on their own, within a scary space that they now know even the adults in their lives don't know how to navigate. And this is the moment that fear becomes contagious. Just like the common cold, the closer we are, the higher the probability that we will be coughing tomorrow.

You might say, "Everyone experiences fear." And you would be correct. However, everyone's actions are not dramatically altered by fear. There are people who fear leaving their homes (This is called Agoraphobia). To many of us, this is unimaginable and a bit of an exaggerated response to fear because we can't imagine being so afraid to walk out of our door that we make the decision to never do it again, but there are people who find that very logical. People who have such anxiety about all the negative possibilities that lie outside their door; that they believe this to be their only solution. And this is just one example of the difference between experiencing fear and having fear alter your existence, which is the fine line between nature's emotions and an altered emotional state to be identified as a mental health issue.

I'm a seventies baby: the last of a generation prior to illness completely taking over. Symptoms have always been in attendance but were able to be ignored. For those who are unhealthy, it's often not until symptoms become debilitating that they're taken seriously. As long as one can still do the things they are capable of doing in their day-to-day, one's not often considering what needs to be done to keep it that way.

If I could describe what life was like in my era, I'd say that the village was still very much intact. As children, our neighborhoods were filled with people who engaged daily, acknowledged one another when passing, and paid close attention to what children belonged to whom. Everyone felt a responsibility to one another, and this was shown by the accountability and support that was present. Although I hadn't experienced the physical discipline by way of neighbors that those prior to my years have described in their stories; it was known that if I did wrong in the community and anyone of age witnessed it; my mother would not only be told but I may have even been taken to her on the spot so it could be addressed immediately. This is where the term: "it takes a village" came from. Everyone in the community played a part. Even the law-breakers in the community had a level of principles because it was a natural responsibility to secure the elders, make sure they were not only safe but also be mindful of what you allowed them to witness by way of you. To be honest, I can't be sure if this was completely a product of having principles or self-preservation because the elders were the law in our culture and definitely going to hold you accountable. But regardless of the reason, this standard was set.

Joy was still very prevalent even in the poorest conditions due to the value that we had for the company of one another. So together, we became really creative in how we filled the financial gaps. We were a prideful people. So the bartering system that we operated through was not only a fair exchange but didn't create shame because it lived under our natural law of reciprocation. When I paint this picture of the early 80s and how I grew up, I'm not detailing a culture short of illness; I'm detailing a culture with enough principles intact to maintain functionality within illness. There was a duality that existed because behind all of the structure that I described still stood the very thin line between discipline and abuse by way of elders, drug dealing and drug consumption at alarming rates, clashes for respect that resulted in the loss of life etc. And regardless of all the previously described comradery taking place at the time, behind that beautiful wallpaper was a fungus growing in the form of generations upon generations of children being sexually assaulted in their homes, in neighbors' homes, with family friends etc. And amongst all those supposedly principled people, this was a secret willing to be kept by entire families and today is still a secret willing to be kept by an entire culture.

Throughout all the symptoms that are spoken of within black culture, it's interesting to hear the crafty ways in which we have been able to explain each symptom making it more digestible for those starving for a way to make it taste better on their tongue. Violence, drug dealing, and consumption, even the value of "things" above human life, tend to fall beneath the scope of survival, but the one symptom that gets stuffed way in the back of the closet due to the lack of a crafty explanation, and an abundance of accountability is childhood sexual assault. Trying to make sense of this symptom will only further expose how sick one is, so it falls beneath the guides of: "Don't air family's dirty laundry." But we are going to air some laundry today!

Why are we so adamant about the rule: "what happens in this house stays in this house"?

What's the real secret, huh?

Is the secret that we are more aware of our illness than we let on, and the shame of this fact creates cultural agreements that allow for us to blend in without notice? Appear to be well? Keep our packaging intact? If so, the cat is out of the bag and has been for a very long time. What happens in the house has been spilling into the streets for years. And when it's not spilling out by way of talk, it's spilling out via triggers and behaviors—symptoms.

We have a saying that goes: "Everything that happens in the dark will come to light." And as current slang would have it, "it's litt!" We are in the spotlight. Front and center, running a muck at a time when we have more visibility, more options, and more financially sound black people than ever. You would think the culture would look a lot different under these circumstances; however, nothing outside of us will fill the void within. We had household names as renowned as Oprah Winfrey breaking her silence. And your average young ladies spilling their tea on TikTok, for the world to see… It's time!

The term blood is thicker than water no longer holds the weight it once did because we are finally at a point where even within the family construct, people are coming in contact with the ill and coming to the conclusion that it's every man/woman for themselves. The black sheep of each family seems to be simultaneously pushing back on the cultural norms to enforce change.

And everyone is going into their own corners.

However: mass separation isn't the answer. Enforcing solitary confinement on ourselves also falls beneath the survival umbrella and further invests in mental illness, which is not what's needed or wanted. We want to thrive. Those who understand life: understand that humans were not made to be separate. A part of mental health is interacting/ relationships. So although I support quarantining to maintain your health from those who are ill, we must find actual solutions to the illness that allows us to move forward in a natural state. We can no longer run and hide from it or ignore it as if it doesn't exist. It's vital for us to start the process towards healthier days for our young rising behind us.

Healthier practices are based upon accountability, showing value for loved ones, having the hard conversations, protecting those whom we hold dear, and facing those who have wronged us. And not placing a label upon anything for the purpose of creating a narrative for comfort; while running from confrontation and claiming to be protecting one's peace. Peace comes by way of dealing with the tough stuff so that they no longer affect our lives negatively in the future – that's peace.

Many may hear the issues being identified in this book and believe them to be society based, and not necessarily a black culture issue. To that, I will say that the issues being addressed are not synonymous with black culture, but they are detrimental to black culture. Much of what's being explained is the swapping of values from one culture to another, and this is what has landed us here. Being black is to value the living, and all that cultivates the evolution of life/ spirit, faith, and love. And none of what has been presented falls beneath that understanding. To reduce anyone to the lack of choice is barbaric, and to wound our young is to wound our people as a whole.

Black culture has combined with the culture of capitalism which holds money and possessions at the top of the priority list but that's another conversation. The point is that two opposites can't exist at once without one canceling the other out. Therefore black culture doesn't look like black culture because it isn't. And black people aren't acting in our natural state because we aren't. I made a prior example using schizophrenia, making the point of symptoms being normal once related to illness but abnormal if no illness exists. The practices I've brought up are symptoms of a larger issue. And very similar to schizophrenia, the voices in our heads speaking against the very things that will breed happiness and healthiness within; are showing the glaring need for a tune-up.

With that being said, I have to point out the fact that black culture, as toxic and misdirected as it stands, is at the forefront of societal trends, and so when our toxicity plays out, it's not only on display for the world's view, but it's available for consumption. And although we are undeniably sick with the disease of the mind, we are also undeniably the blueprint for cool, and who doesn't want to consume that?

To acknowledge this as a fact, we must also acknowledge that black wellness benefits everyone. Well, at least those who don't benefit from our ailment. Our need for healing is evident! And the growing amounts of people identifying with depression, anxiety etc. exposes it most. We are a people who inherently have a high tolerance for pain. By the time we cry out, we have likely already endured more pain than anyone else would be able to bear. So these cries are also a showing of a cultural emergency.

To be clear, I am no doctor and never claimed to be; however, it's not rocket science for me to be able to identify patterns that show up as symptoms of an illness. We have all grown up understanding that a runny nose and cough are symptoms of a common cold, but if paired with greater symptoms such as hot and cold flashes and muscle aches, it just may be the flu. Doctors may be the only ones in our society whose conclusions are deemed credible to give diagnoses, but we are all aware that they aren't the only ones who can identify illness.

We identify illness prior to visiting a physician; that's what leads us to the doc's office in the first place. As we walk through the trail of wounds identifying the many sources of suffering, we will also identify and explore the many symptoms that are a tell-tell that illness is among us. So we can treat a culture in the hot zone of an epidemic: one symptom at a time!

CHAPTER 11

The Trail of Evidence

When I began walking this path, I was completely unaware as to where it would lead, but I knew that I had already made up my mind that I would trust the process no matter where it took me. And I was led here; go figure! No one could have convinced me prior to being in this moment that my purpose wasn't creating and curating a beautiful, legendary work of art by way of one of the many art forms that I frequent. It seems that I was only partially correct. Art would be the vehicle, but health and wellness would be the purpose. I spent a large chunk of life asking God, the universe, source; whatever you'd like to call it, "why me?"

Being this kid, whose wounds presented as silence due to the knowledge of uninhibited speech going against the laws in my home; led to my body being ravished as my mouth remained shut without screams to bring attention to the bruises. Only sirens rang as my fist became loud, fighting against the many restrictions my spirit felt. When I lost the only person who enjoyed the space of my voice, the sound of my words, and the depth of my mind to the hands of another sick man; by way of murder. I died another death! While this other me resides in this body that just wouldn't conform to social norms that didn't quite fit its social measurements, I'd ask: "why?"

I was constantly questioning myself as if I was the model that needed a recall because I just wasn't working the way I was told I was supposed to. This then led to me trying to fix what I believed to be broken and could only be put back together by some dude who could possibly change my mind: but it wouldn't change! Leading to pregnancy at the age of fourteen and officially a mom at the age of fifteen. Why? The more that I tried to fix, the more I seemed to break.

The world understood what was special, but me, I only saw a tool to help me cope with the hell that I existed in. When The High School of Arts & Design accepted me, I was a freshman with a belly whose hump blocked my vision, making me short-sighted. Becoming pretty good at living this duality that I picked up along the way made it easy to be the best rapper in the lunchroom, the knockout artist at dismissal, and mom when I got home. The facade was the why! But as long as I made sure to keep a poetic verse bouncing from my pen to a page that would house all of these thoughts, feelings, and plans, I knew I'd be free at some point. Only when I got kicked out of my mother's house would I be able to put this plan to the test, and test it was. If you think loneliness is the lack of company, try being alone with only your thoughts and a child relying on those thoughts to keep them safe and sound when you have yet to feel safe and sound on your own.

This was just the beginning of what began the cycle of mental illness that fell upon me. I won't go into depth about my life because that's for another book; however, I will say that the events that began to take place later were the result of how I internalized all that took place prior. I wasn't at fault for being silenced in my home; I wasn't at fault for being sexually violated; I wasn't at fault for my best friend getting murdered! Nor was I at fault for being gay, black, or affected by it all. What was my fault was allowing fear to cage my voice when I needed it most, allowing myself to believe that I had no choice but to deal with all of these thoughts and feelings alone.

Like many others, I had people around, but my trust issues made me feel as if I didn't. The world is as we believe it to be, and so alone I was. Every choice made thereafter was curated by a mind that no longer thought logically, so one can imagine that it got rough. I got in the ring as an opponent to life and life whooped my ass! Every time I took a blow, life took fault because accountability wasn't my corner-man. I fought back, but we had it out, and life won, closing out the match by raising its arms as it looked down at my lifeless body, finally in a state of surrender.

We all have huge hurdles in our lives, and no one is exempt. And yes, some of us are dealt what we believe to be harder hands than others but it's life. So I had to train differently. Everything is mental, so I had to think differently. And fight for my peace.

While speaking to people about the approach to healing via the "Wounded project; I've gotten feedback such as:

"It's hard!"

"You don't understand!"

"I try…"

"Everyone deals with things differently!"

"Everyone isn't you!"

The many crafty ways that we package saying: "it's too hard, I don't want to." No one ever promised anything would be easy. But what I will say is that it is worth it! As someone who has worked through massive amounts of trauma for no other reason other than to be better, the only thing I don't understand is: not wanting to be better. The goal is wellness, happiness, and harmony, so if you try and have yet to succeed: proceed until reaching the goal. After all, where's the better option?

These things are said to me as if I speak from a place of lacking understanding, and I don't know anyone who understands it more! As I said, I haven't always been well. I reflect on many moments from my past and think of how mentally ill I was to respond and think in the ways that I once did. So I am aware of the difficulty, and I'm not presenting anyone with any steps that I haven't personally taken. Once you're well, it's understood that there are amends to make, and a great part of healing is making amends. Because, as they say, misery really does love company. However, so does happiness. And I can honestly say that finding my happy place has enforced this need to introduce happiness to others.

So I understand that everyone deals with things differently, but our focus should be to deal with things healthily, and this is what "Wounded" is about.

Last but not least, I'm well aware that everyone isn't me; in fact, no one but me is me. But the same can be said for you; therefore, the statement is counter-productive. Let's build a legacy of health together.

There are stages to illness, and we are experiencing them all. The early stage of illness is often said to be the lucky stage: Lucky because this is when the illness has been identified before it becomes problematic. We were in this stage way back in the 80s, and I remember being warned by powerful voices within the culture who identified not only the external threats but the internal threats to be addressed. And I can recollect them clearly. In fact, I know that I was meant to experience voices such as Sista Soulja and many others for this exact moment. Although it seems that those powerful messages had fallen upon deaf ears, the fact that the seed that these voices planted back then has blossomed into what is being established via "Wounded" today speaks to the ability of one seed to save the crop season.

The second stage, although not early, isn't yet in the red zone. It's the stage that's known to be the treatment and/ or maintenance stage. We've shown our level of severity in this stage with the rise of suicide and public outcry in the black community growing by 30% in 2014 (Congressional Black Caucus. Ring the alarm: the crisis of Black youth suicide in America. Accessed December 29, 2020.)

Last but definitely not least, is the stage that requires a face-to-face discussion about the severity of the illness and what that means.

This book is our face-to-face!

Feelings of despair are taking over, and many are trying to find the words to express where they stand mentally and emotionally. Depression has become the word used when people experience sadness, although it's so much deeper. Anxiety has become the word used when one experiences nervousness, although we all experience this at some point. Many words have lost their luster due to being used out of context, especially when it comes to words that represent diagnosis.

I understand that many of us may be suffering from these afflictions; however, in order to be accurately diagnosed, an expert on mental illness must look over your mental and emotional states before concluding what it is that one is suffering with. Language is important in every realm. It's the method for comprehension and communication. Without knowledge of the definitions of words in each space; understanding is not possible. So when these terms are used incorrectly, it becomes harder to identify those who really suffer from these afflictions. Which makes it harder to see illness for what it is.

Definition Submission:

Depression is actually: a mental condition characterized by feelings of severe hopelessness, discouragement, feelings of inadequacy, and guilt, that often alters energy, appetite, and sleep. It's much more than just having a bad day.

And anxiety is actually: a nervous disorder characterized by a state of excessive uneasiness and apprehension, typically with compulsive behavior or panic attacks. Being nervous is normal; it only crosses the normality lines once it alters your state of being.

And the word crazy means: mentally deranged. And it's used way too freely.

Everyone has some level of trauma in their past, but not everyone is stuck there. Everyone is nervous to some degree about what the future holds, but not everyone is focused there. The described afflictions are caused by the inability to be present.

"If you are depressed, you are living in the past. If you are anxious, you are living in the future. If you are at peace, you are living in the present."

-Lao Tzu

Harmony and peace is the goal! And because my goal is to create solutions for the issues that have affected us as a culture. I would be lost not to address the responsibility I feel to paint a picture that expresses a visual outlook on the deterioration of our health via our culture, the lack of healthy habits within the culture, and how this became the wounds that are to be addressed in our current state. Behaviors identify symptoms of something greater. And just because there are large numbers of people behaving a certain way, please don't be confused as to believe that the amount of people moving within the same pattern equates to whether something comes by way of nature or circumstance. It just may be a reflection of Normalized Trauma. To be clear consensus is that a large part of black culture today is founded upon mental illness and trauma response. Black culture is trauma culture, but it no longer has to be.

There's the emotion of things, then the facts of things we must be able to identify which is which.

This entire experience: from living the trauma, and healing, to maintaining my health and the creation of

The colors of Pain: Wounded

Wounded, enforced the need to dissect my thoughts and understandings for the purpose of establishing which came by way of trauma versus what came by way of understanding healthy interactions. I had to really put things in their rightful folder for the purpose of being fair. There was so much that was hidden that, through this process, has been revealed, and I now know that the path laid prior to today has been preparing me for all that I need to know at this moment. Knowing and doing are very different, and the execution of what you believe yourself to know is the key.

There are many exchanges that take place in our younger years. And those exchanges include intimacy that isn't really discussed. The stage of experimenting to get an understanding of one's sexuality is a part of that. From ages 10-13, most young people have had some level of experimentation with a peer and come to the conclusion that they either like or could do without that exchange until their later years. This can be as little as a kiss, touching, or more. Although many don't tell the adults about it, youth are getting their own data to form their own opinions. And although we like to forget who we were as children, we did too! It's important for us to be able to identify the natural progression of sexuality and have the necessary discussions with our young that educate them and bring clarity to their thoughts and feelings in this area. Many of us were moving blindly, figuring it out on our own, which led to many horror stories or misinformation, but we are responsible for creating the understanding of what is natural versus what is a violation of their natural progression.

While writing this book, my daughter told me for the very first time about a couple of sexual exchanges that came by way of youth. My trauma immediately demonized the exchange before taking the details into account. Many of us have a hard time seeing our children as sexual beings, and I'm no different. The point is they are. And they aren't going to be children forever. As parents, our job is to inform, guide, and be an example for which they can follow, so although she's now an adult informing me of her experience, I had to remind myself that I am still her example for how she will deal with her young during their exploration stage. And that understanding brought forth an entirely different mindset when speaking with her about sex and guiding her in the conversation she's preparing to have with her pre-teen.

CHAPTER 12

A False Report

Myths: "Time heals all wounds."

The truth is that wounds often only heal without leaving a scar when treated. And those who hide behind such statements are fearful of what it takes to get to a place of healing.

"Standing with those that you care for whether right or wrong is loyalty."

Loyalty isn't represented by one's tie to people; loyalty is displayed by way of accountability. One is loyal to those they have a level of care for, and if one cares, they want the best for… therefore loyalty is holding loved ones accountable for their rights and wrongs. Be loyal to what's right!

"Adversity breaks you."

Adversity, although difficult, is often what builds your foundation for durability and growth.

"Love hurts"

Love doesn't hurt at all. It can sometimes be uncomfortable because with love comes accountability and honesty: but pain and discomfort are two very different things. The actions of someone who claims to love you but doesn't act in love aren't reflections of actual love. Don't give love a bad rap due to the actions of people.

"Love is a feeling"

Love is much more than a feeling. It's substantial: it's actual. It's a series of constant actions to support feelings. If one cannot define love, one does not know love and therefore cannot live it.

"You were born alone."

We are awarded to parents and whether or not those parents were capable of being the caretakers they were put in place to be is another conversation, but we weren't born alone. We start this life with a support system, and with the building of relationships, we are supposed to grow our support system. Those who lean on such statements are responding to the fear of being disappointed again.

"Vulnerability is weak"

Actually, vulnerability is a superpower! Yes, you can get hurt while vulnerable, but you can also get hurt while guarded. The difference is that lacking vulnerability and closing oneself off may also result in blocking not just painful exchanges but blissful ones.

"Life is hard"

Life is what we make it! I found that although there are events that are out of our control, when we choose what we do control wisely, and respond healthily to the events in our lives. It really does move pretty smoothly. Life isn't hard at all under those conditions.

"We fall in love"

We don't fall in love; we rise in love. When in a healthy loving exchange, it builds, lifts, secures and reciprocates. There's no falling there.

"Blood is thicker than water."

If we were speaking literally, I'd have to agree, but since this quote is a play on family vs. everyone else, it must be clarified that if you have a healthy family dynamic, the statement can or may be true; however, blood family is not inherently more solid than others. The family we choose may be much more solid.

Don't allow phrases like this to persuade the necessary choices made to build your village.

"You can just snap out of a mental health issue."

I'm sure we wish that were the case but it takes a great deal of work, tools, support, and often professional help to maintain wellness.

"Mental and physical health are separate."

Actually, mental, physical and emotional health are linked. Poor mental health can impact physical health, and this connection works both ways.

"We should refrain from having expectations because they will get you hurt."

Actually, we should expect the people in our lives to stick to their agreements, but if we expect things that haven't been agreed upon, we set ourselves up for failure.

"Trust and respect are earned"

This mindset also comes from a place of fear. No one should start with a deficit. We should all begin with a full cup unless our steps cause a spill. Trust and respect are given until lost. Not earned!

"Isolation is where growth takes place."

To look inward doesn't take isolation, and because isolation takes away the challenge component that is necessary when we come to our own conclusions, it can often stunt growth. In order to solidify a belief, it must be able to survive questions and challenges; therefore growth happens with the trading of thoughts, questions, and theories of others.

"Honesty is rude."

To be rude is to be offensive, although the truth can be a bit painful. It's not rude; it's necessary for the ability to be well informed and make conscious choices.

"Tone determines the respect of what's said."

The reality is that different cultures, families etc. express themselves with different tones, and it's not always a reflection of intention, mood, or respect. So there are so many other factors to take into account before concluding that someone has ill will.

"Real men don't cry"

Not only do real men cry, but all genuine life forms feel and respond to emotion which isn't weakness nor strength; it's a part of our natural makeup. For emotion to be frowned upon is for humanity to be frowned upon.

"Hurt people hurt people"

Although there's something to this statement, we all have been hurt on some level, and we don't all pass the pain on. Hurt people who have not identified, acknowledged, and begun their process of healing their pain hurt people. It's very important to be specific.

"Everything isn't black and white."

This is correct; however, all solutions come by way of black and white. If we are headed in the direction of solution instead of sitting within the problem, black and white is the standard for better.

The colors of Pain: Wounded

THE ART OF WOUNDS

Before wounds, there is a clean slate.

Scarless laughter painted with the beauty of pureness as emotions is intact.

Transparency by nature, truth without regard—innocence—is what wounds DON'T look like!

Wounds filthy the slate, tamper with laughter, take the pureness of emotion and mix it all up: until one has no idea what they feel and why?

Wounds can confuse others as it creates interesting abstracts with colorful bruising that speak to art, all while tainting the water—the dirty water—won't be clear until the brushes are clean.

We look in the mirror matching the scars with outfits as we have been deemed intricate in our mess.

if healed, will they see us less?

These wounds now pop culture applaud my inner vulture, fighting to maintain its umph!

I walk in rooms, and umph!

They see, they flock: this umph!

The colors of Pain: Wounded

These wounds are beauty until they bleed all over you

Then the mess is

the message

And my art loses value

And my intent is to convince you that I just tried style you

No more looking in the mirror

Because these scars now clearer

I have nothing to wear

These wounds don't match my hair

these wounds don't go with these clothes

Time to get a new look I suppose…HEAL!

Poem by

Kamisha Oliver/ MahagonyB

www.ingramcontent.com/pod-product-compliance
Lightning Source LLC
Chambersburg PA
CBHW062052290426
44109CB00027B/2802